The Universal Laws
and the
Natural Laws
of the
Western Hemisphere

———

JAMES ROSS

The Universal Laws and the Natural Laws of the Western Hemisphere

© 2020 by James Ross

Table of Contents

Chapter 1| Polar Motion

We will begin to see the divine harmony of nature's grandest law, which causes every portion of our earth's surface to become alternately a fruitful plain or a barren waste, dry land, or ocean bed.

The earth's pole moves in one uniform direction with a slow, imperceptible motion that forms a spiral path in the heavens. This consists of small spiral orbits or circles, one overlapping the other. These small spiral circles are termed "volutes," their true value in space being three degrees 36 minutes and zero seconds.

The motion of inclination of the pole is at the rate of 50 seconds of space per century or one second in every two years. At this rate, it requires 7,200 years to move over one degree. There are 360 degrees in a circle or the pole's orbit; it takes 360 times 7,200 years to equal 2,592,000 years to make a complete revolution of its orbit or 100 solar years.

Again, each volute is three degrees 36 minutes and zero seconds in true value, so 25,920 years are required for the pole to complete one small spiral. There are exactly 100 of these spiral orbits in the

complete orbit, therefore, 100 times 25,290 years
equals 2,592,000 years. One polar day equals 100 sun
years.

EXAMPLES OF POLAR MOTION

Imagine our earth's pole to be perpendicular
to the plane of its orbit and consequently coinciding
with the pole of the ecliptic, then the signs of the
zodiac and apparent yearly path of the sun's will
always be vertical at our earth's equator. Hence, the
universal spring will reign in the temperate zones and
a gentle continuous summer in all sub-tropical
latitudes will cause the equatorial regions of the earth
to become blazing, scorching deserts. The Great
Plains will be unfit for habitation, owing to the fierce
rays of a vertical sun continuing for long ages.
However, the dream state of man will be the seat of
human life. This condition will also cause equal day
and night all over the globe.

Why is it that our polar regions will have a
tropical summer? Each year, the sun will be vertical
on the 21st of June to the North Pole and on the 21st
of December to the South Pole. Every portion of the

globe with the sun and earth's pole in this position will witness a tropical summer and an artic winter.

The walls of the mighty Babylon and the eight-volved tower of Babel or cloud-encompassed Bel were never constructed to resist any mortal foe. Those city walls (which were 60 miles in circumference, 200 feet high, and 578 feet thick), were not made to defy the strength of armies, but to resist the fearful forces of nature. This includes the floods that swept the plains of truth from the mountains of America every spring during this age of horror.

The tremendous embankments and river walls constructed by the ancients are monuments of human skill and enterprise belonging to an epoch that antedates by thousands of years the age of the supposed builders. These mighty old monuments are indeed the sacred relics of our early forefathers, but modern historians are so bound by the biblical chronology that they cannot see the light. Like young puppies, their eyes will not open to the light until they are nine days old.

The student here is requested to notice that all the great solar and lunar observatories were constructed for a two-fold purpose—their religion—

unlike that of their degenerated descendants was a pure scientific theology or Wisdom Religion.

Remember that the great Polar Day of 2,592,000 years moves once around like the index of the clock determines the duration upon our planet of that vital spiritual impulse of evolution. It is known as the great life-wave. This life-wave passes around the catenary chain or circuit of the seven planets not in an even, regular or continuous action, but in waves or impulses.

It must be known, in the first place, that there are Seven Kingdoms, Seven Principles, and Seven Ruling Powers in nature. Matter is the most remote expression of spirit. The Seven Kingdoms are the three elemental and invisible, and the four objective and visible planes of nature. The order of the seven principles or forms evolution are:

1) *Spiritual*
2) *The Astral*
3) *The Gaseous*
4) *The Mineral*
5) *The Vegetable*
6) *The Animal*
7) *The Human*

The Seven Governors, or powers, ruling a planet are the Seven Angelic States. There is neither accident nor any such thing as chance in this life or the worlds beyond. All external things and events are the result of internal causes and there are arc rules by which they can be forecasted and anticipated.

By this, we do not mean that all human events and occurrences are foreseen by the ancestors of this world we inhabit and who for redemptive (or other ends) may reveal many things to their worthy protégés. We mean that within this universe there is a great central source of intelligences, power, presence, and energy, which necessarily knows all that was, is, and is to be.

This central power must be environed by extent mental energies and potentialities in knowledge only second to its Supreme Self. We do not conceive such potencies to be ascended human beings who once dwelt in physical bodies, lived, died, and rose again.

There are electrical, ethereal, and non-material universes far grander, vaster, and more magnificent that this of ours with all its amazing systems and stretch of fathomless eternities than this of ours is superior to an anthill. There are legions of hierarchies, potencies, powers, and intelligences not of human material genesis before whose amazing sweep of mind is the grandest intellect earth ever has or can produce is as a pebble to a mountain range. These beings are the arbiters of the destinies of the worlds and the originators of the grand drama of external life.

The capacity of deity is boundless; that of man is limited and is either vast contracted in strict accordance with the relative-ratio of his soul development or independence of mere bodily senses personal or material bias. Perfect development means perfect at-one-ment (atonement). This is the sacrifice of the lower nature upon the cross of purification and evolution of the true Christ within. The real Christian beyond all creeds exists only in the truly perfected man.

One who's developed can place himself en-rapport with the centers of celestial life, traverse the spaces, and penetrate the Grand Arcana of the universe itself. Man has not omniscience, but has much penetration; he is not omnipotent yet possesses enormous latent powers. He cannot be omnipresent but is capable of being everywhere that is of being mentally and spiritually in many places and seen at the same time.

The human body is, in its more interior sense, the mystical uterus of Isis. The human body is the uterus of nature and is ever pregnant with the Holy Spirit (or incarnated soul). When the period of gestation is completed, the cycle of evolution shall give birth to the Son of God whose kingdom is not of this earth, but of Heaven. That is, of course, the soul, which has attained its immortality. The Son of God's future state of being is the boundless realm of spirit.

I and the father are one, meaning the human body is but an atom of the father. This at-one-ment is the mystical at-one-ment of the Christ Spirit within the human soul of man. The man who cannot love is an inhuman monster. There is nothing human about him except the outward physical form of humanity, which is but the dust or flesh that your spirit is in. It inwardly conceals the ravenous wolf within because the lack of identity with your true self.

It is only the true human that can truly love and, in loving, let their soul transcend all lower passions. Lust is not love; lust is the animal or passionate appetite with nothing human about it and woe be those whose love cannot rise above the plane of lust. The soul cannot live healthy or evolve to its powers where the tainted mildew of either lust or an impure life is allowed to remain. If powers are developed in such a state, they are abnormal and impure. They are mere fungi of the soul because they are forced and reared under artificial conditions, and are consequently liable to wither up and die on exposure to the first blighting currents of the Astral light when disastrous results always follow.

The student should know it is both Heaven and ultimate glories of eternal progression, or it is hell and ruination with the terrible surroundings of the black magician. There is almost a certainty of final extinction in the elementary spheres of the soul worlds.

The virgin womb shall give birth to the immortal Son of God when the period of gestation is completed. This is also the great cycle of necessity; you must be born again or you cannot enter the kingdom of Heaven.

The vaporous gas, while incarnated in the physical organism, is within the womb of nature. It is only when its full time has come and it has gained its immortality that it is reborn into the realms of spirit. It has burst the bonds of flesh and blood escaped from its mother's womb. All those who lose their immortality are simply the miscarriages of human nature.

SELF-MASTERY

Self-mastery consists first of a perfect mastery of the individual's own soul. No advance whatsoever can be made in acquiring power over other spirits such as controlling the lower or supplicating the higher until the spirit within has acquired such perfect mastery of itself. It can never be moved to anger or emotion, realizes no pleasure, cares for no pain, and experiences no mortification at insult, loss or disappointment. It subdues every emotion that stirs common men's minds. To arrive at this state, continued discipline is necessary.

Having acquired this perfect equilibrium, the next step is power. The individual must be able to wake when he pleases and sleep where he will. He must, by virtue, of complete subjugation of his earthly nature be able to invoke planetary and even solar spirits and commune with them to a certain degree.

To attain these degrees of power, the processes are so difficult that a man or woman can scarcely become one and yet continue his relations with his fellowmen. He must continue, from the first to the last degree, a long series of exercises. Each of them must be perfected before another is undertaken.

A practical spiritualist may be of either sex, but must observe as the first law (pure self-control) and that with a view of conserving all the energetic powers of the body. No aged person—especially one who has not lived the life of strict self-control—can acquire the full sum of the powers above named.

It is better to commence practice in early youth; for after the meridian of life when the processes of waste prevail over repair, few of the powers above described can be attained, the full sum never.

Chapter 2 | *The Six Days of Creation*

The preceding five tide-wave of evolution has now prepared our earth for nature's grandest climax—the evolution of the human form—man.

The Bible says, "And the Lord made man out of the dust of the ground and breathed into his nostrils the breath of life and he became a living soul and the Lord created man in his own image. Male and female, he created them."

During the five days of creation, the vegetable and animal evolved. When man appears in the scene, everything is in a vastly improved and highly developed condition compared with the condition of the earthly monstrous forms. The missing link or first human forms the connection between the animal and human. It was caused by a spiritual union, which, acting upon the highest form of animal, an ape—for example—produced an entirely different species quite human in their organism but hairy, etc. From this missing link, the human was evolved, but this is erroneous and void of truth.

While the spirit atoms have been evolving upward, as mentioned in Genesis, each day is one

Polar Day. As stated before, this is 2,592,000 years of earthly time. The words "the evening" are mentioned first and "the morning" last; this is correct. The dark or undeveloped portion of each wave is the first half and signifies symbolically night and vice versa.

Further, it must be remembered that the spiritual impulse or wave must pass around the future planet before anything can transpire. It is the divine will sent forth by the spirit-state that is equivalent to the word or divine idea of certain ancient writers.

This fiat attracts within its orbit the latent cosmic matter of space and transforms it into the embryonic nebulous light, the start dust, or radiant fire mist, which is the form or primitive matter of all creation.

The student must strictly remember that there is no specific duration of this state. It may last for millions of ages before the actual evolution of a planet. Previous to the symbolical six days of creation, this planet exists for untold cycles in a nebulous condition the exact size of its orbital ring.

THE FIRST DAY OF CREATION

The Supreme Angelic Governors project into active evolution the Astral tide-wave, the currents of

Astral Light, and the nebulous matter is at once transformed into a rapidly revolving globe of fire, which solidifies and cools under the intense concentration of the Deific Will of the Governors in a wonderfully less space of time than any of our transcendental or spiritual writers can imagine.

Fire was dominant for the first half of the Polar Day. Its surface had become so far cooled as to allow the heated vapors of its immense atmosphere to condense and form water, which element was rapidly produced during the next half of the cycle. Thus, we see that a rude globe was formed during the first half of the evening, and was given to the dominion of fire alone. The latter half or morning was one ceaseless war between those opposing elements like fire and water. These two periods of the Polar Cycle are each 1,296,000 years, and were called by the Hindus the Treta Yug.

THE SECOND DAY OF CREATION

The Supreme Angelic Governors now caused the first evolution of the Gaseous or Chemical tide-wave and the evolution of a complete but dense atmosphere was the result. The various constituents of the atmosphere were by this wave adjusted and our planet's chemical affinities duly balanced. This caused the whole of the super-abundant gross matter such as carbon, etc., to condense and fall to the surface of the planet.

Also during this day, our planet's surface was the scene of a continual conflict between heat and water. It was the scene of mighty volcanic actions; mountain ranges continually rose and fell, and ocean beds were always shifting.

THE THIRD DAY OF CREATION

After the gaseous/the great mineral tide-wave commenced, the spirit atoms of future egos became incarnated in dense matter for the first time. It was namely in the strata of rocks and mineral lodes, which constitute the land above the ocean level sank and the ocean became dry land. For the first time, the seas and oceans occupied their proper beds, and the evening and morning were the third day.

It must be added that during this period also, the planet's surface was the scene of continual volcanic action, as was each and every period. At the close of the Polar Cycle, we see that the evolution of the Astral, chemical, and mineral waves have now prepared our earth for the first vegetable forms of life. The first forms of all things were born and had their origin in water.

THE FOURTH DAY OF CREATION

The vegetable tide-wave now reaches the barren shores of our planet and produces the first rudimental forms of vegetable life. This, in turn, develops the most gross, gigantic shapes that are rude and imperfect as the earth upon which they grow. But as time progresses, so do the vegetable kingdom, each age giving more perfect forms.

THE FIFTH DAY OF CREATION

With the previous tide-waves having run their course, the animal life-wave now sets in and forms the lowest rudimental forms of life while successively evolving the various orders of animal life race after race. As it runs its course and becomes extinct, and gives place to more complete organisms, the mineral and spiritual forms involved downward until it became intangible and objective. It possessed at first, a vast but loosely organized body.

Each age saw it smaller and more compact until, at the end of the third race of the first human round, the spiritual man had a compact and well-organized body and the commencement of the fourth race. The center of the seven was the first point of contact, the focus of the spirit downward, and the development of the mental upwards. Matter and spirit met and formed the first real physical man of the human race.

This is the Great Mystery; the lowest point in the arc of spiritual involution infringes upon the highest arc or culminating point of the dream state of man. The evolution of the remaining root races begins to ebb and slowly quits our shores, and our earth, for the first time, enjoy a rest.

Chapter 3 | The Key

The author of the key thought in far grander periods of time than they had the religious teachers of today. They determined that each of the Seven Angels would rule 12 times during one great solar period of 25, 920 years. Each would govern the world in turn for about 308 years and 208 ½ days, and the seven together would complete one round of governance in 2,160 years the time it takes the sun to pass through one sign of the zodiac.

As is made clear in the companion work "The Hermectic Key," even these large numbers is only the beginning and the succession of cycles is never-ending. The significance of the exercise given in "The Key" presumably obtained by adjusting the starting points was to demonstrate the uniqueness of the year 1881. The strength of the Cosmic Forces behind the revival of the exterior circle of the order from 2,438 B.C. is 4,320 years before 1881. This was a period precisely equal to the time it took the sun to pass through Aries and Pisces, and enter Aquarius.

It dated the transition to Aquarius to December 1880 or February 1881 and taught that, at that time, the Iron Age of Sam, the Angel of Mars gave way to the Enlightened Age of Micheal the Sun God. Micheal had presided at the initial formation of the interior circle and at the birth of Christ. In 1881, it would usher in the age of the renewal of spirituality and the destruction of Sacredotalism and tyranny.

The correct order of succession is the natural order of planetary application. The Angel/Intelligence of Saturn receives power and after ruling the world for 308 years (208 ½ days) resigns the government to the Angel of Jupiter who stands second in the order of the ruling powers. After another term of 308 years (208 ½ days), it hands over the control of the Angel of Mars, who, for the same period subjects the world and its inhabitants to the influence of martial force.

Then, in the fourth order of the Seven Governors, Archangel Micheal, the center and also the Chief of the Seven Principles retired in favor of the next succession. The fifth order, whose name is Prince of the Astral Light and Chief Angel of the Planet Venus, retired and received the scepter of earthly rule. The swift messenger of the gods and presiding intelligence of the planet, Mercury, rules for 308 years (208 ½ days).

The negative receives the ruling powers. The intelligence, which is the Angel of the Moon, governs the earth for 308 years (208 ½ days). It is the seventh and last of the order, and this completes the sub-solar cycle of 2,160 years. The cycle takes command once more and so on, cycle after cycle.

A brief glance into past history will be instructive to the student of psychology and to enable him to do this and assist his researches. We supply the following correct data terminating a sub-solar cycle with Archangel Michael, receiving the government of the world in the beginning of the year 1881 when the sub-races of the Western Hemisphere reach the equator of human progress. We carry our researches forward from this date up to the culminating point of the arc, from which point Western Races descend the cycle and once more relapse into ignorance.

The student must bear in mind that there are three different kinds of cycles spoken of.
The first are solar-cycles, thus 25,920 years through the twelve signs of the zodiac and consequently completing one revolution of this orbit around the center. It is the twelfth part of the Great Cycle and the period of the sun passing though one sign of the zodiac equals to 30 degrees of space. When the sun

has passed through one sign, he has completed one sub-cycle and the new sub-cycle dates from his entry into a fresh sign.

For Example: the sun, at the end of the year A.D. 1880, left the sign Pisces and entered Aquarius. The sun's motion through space is exactly the reverse of the natural order of the zodiacal signs, from Aries to Taurus, and so on. From this, it will be seen that the sun, in 1881, began a new sub-cycle and that the order of succession of the Seven Governors is such that Archangel Micheal governs the first term of each sign. Therefore, by the time Archangel Micheal works around again, the sun will be entering Capricorn.

The second kind of cycle is the period of the Seven Governors that, although exactly of 2,160 years, it is not measured by signs or constellations. It neither begins nor terminates with the sub-cycle, but is measured. Thus, it forms the commencement of Saturn's rule) to the termination of the (Moon's rule) is one complete period or cycle.

The third kind of a cycle is the Arc of Human Progress. Mental and physical alternately carries a race of people (or an empire) to the summit of power and civilization. It goes down again in spite of itself to the greatest depths of ignorance; the duration of this cycle varies considerably according to the kind of race it affects. The great period is the duration or reign of the Seven Root Races of each round.

Next, was the duration of a single root race. Lastly, the duration of each of the numerous offshoot races belongs to the seven branches and their minor sub-races. In any case, the arc moves in the same harmonious order, while obeying the divine impulse of the seven eternal principles of nature, evolving its energies in great mighty waves when ruling the earliest root races, and comprising hundreds of thousands of years in a single period.

The year 1881 may appear incorrect to anyone conversant with modern astronomy, which maintains that our sun will not enter the sign Aquarius until the year A.D. 1897. This is a difference of sixteen years, but modern astronomers are wrong; the sun entered Aquarius in February of 1881. This is not the only mistake they have to discover. The present Great Western Race is one of the seven branches of the fifth root race belonging to the fourth round of evolution. When speaking of the future, glory and fall do not by any means comprise or include the whole Great Western Race. It will be sufficient to say that the US, Great Britain, France, and England may have

taken typical examples of the sub-races therein
referred to several other European races are also
included.

Chapter 4| Symbolical Notes to the First Degree

The student must thoroughly realize that the following is only a very limited outline of a few explanatory symbols in connection with the former M.S.S. The subject is of so vast a nature as to details that many volumes might be written explanatory there unto. This is not for the present, however required, but as the student begins to fully understand the truth.

The sexual emblems everywhere conspicuous in the ancient temples would seem impure in description but no clean and thoughtful mind could regard them, while recognizing the obvious simplicity solemnity and meaning. Such subjects typify when science effectually and unerringly demonstrates to us the origin of matter. It also proves the fallacy of spiritualists and of the aged old ancestors who held as their descendants now hold that matter is but one of the correlations of spirit. Then will the world of prejudiced and vain skeptics have a right to reject the grand old wisdom of the sacred science or throw the charge of obscurity in the teeth of the religions, but not until then, which will be the famous mysteries of Eleusis the Bacchic rites, the feasts in honor of Ceres, the orgies of Cybele and other mythic personages of the Greek pantheon. Ancient Masonry, speculative and operative and its degraded and imbecile descendants, modern Freemasonry have all their origin founded upon the basic principles of these old sex symbols.

Every one of these symbols is an embodied idea combining the conception of the divine invisible with the earthly and visible. Nearly all scriptural names have a direct bearing upon sexual ideas. The names of the 12 tribes bear a direct reference to generative functions.

In connection with this phallic symbolism, it may herein be observed that many things are cognate to each other and are personified under one form. Let it be known that Adam means to be red or blood-covered. The shedding of blood was as much the type of conception as of death. The pictured symbol of this was membrum virile martis generator, also known as Testis and Yoni.

The female pudenda is sacred to Mars, for he held the house of Venus and that of Scorpion. Without the shedding of blood, there is no remission of sin. The Scorpion has the sign of the virgin joined to that of Mars, and the non-sensical rendering of Genesis 3:15 must be apparent to any thoughtful student of sexual symbolism. "I will put enmity between thee and the woman and between thy seed and her seed, it shall bruise thy head and thou shalt bruise his heel."

The word "heel" is an expression substituted as the feet in Isaiah 7:20. See also Jeremiah 8:22 and Nahum 3:5. The part intended to be signified by the word is Pudenda Muliebra; it is also seen that in very ancient Hindu pictures, the heel is highly regarded as touching the mouth of the female sexual organ.

Circumcision, or bloody circle, is a symbol of those significant sex-mysteries and just as the word ZACR or SACR, or carrier of the germ, the special word for the male reproductive organ is translated by male.

The custom was to make the memorial before the Lord with SACR, hence the Latin word sacr-factum of the Roman Priest and the sacrifio, or the English Sacrifice. Just as SACR is related to man's higher existence with another and better realm of life shadowed forth as sacr-ment in the body and blood, bread and wine also symbolized the germ of that existence. Like SACR, bread and wine were also vehicles of its formation.

Cain, in the Bible, is represented as the first murderer, and every fifth man in his descent is also a murderer. Cain, in Hebrew, means a smith or artificer. From this, we have Vul-Cain, who is the personification of the art of ironwork. Tubal-Cain was an instructor of every artificer in brass and iron, and astrologically speaking, the planet Mars rules over such as well as iron. Cain or Mars pierces Abel and the Great Britain sons of Mars pierces Jesus on the cross. The Nazarene is pierced in the left side, just as when the woman is taken from the man's side in the allegorical story of the Garden of Eden.

Horus is also represented, standing in his boat, and piercing the head of the dragon typhoon or Aphophis. The Scandinavian, Thor, bruises the head of the serpent with his cruciform mase. Apollo kills the dragon all unequivocally symbolizing the same ideas, which exist in every country and in every clime. Esau and Jacob are allegorical twins; they're symbols of the ever-present dual principles in nature. In the beginning, God—the Elohim—created man in his own image. Both male and female (father and mother) exists in deity.

Jacob is Israel, who is the left-hand pillar; the feminine principle of Esau the Red, who is the right pillar and male principle. The name of Israel is derived from Isaral or Asar, the Sun-God, also known as Suryad/Surya/Sur. Israel means "strong with God."

Jacob's thigh is dislocated in the wrestling with the angel in the dark and his name is changed to Israel. The sun rising upon Jacob-Israel symbolizes the fecundation of matter or Earth represented by the female Jacob changed to the male Israel. All these symbols speak plainly for themselves for Jehovah, Osiris, Allah, Jah, etc; they are the symbols of the active principle in nature par excellence or the forces, which preside at the formation or regeneration of matter and its dissolution. The two-types of life and death are ever fecundating and ever changing under the ever-existing influx of the Astral Light, which is behind the correlation of the blind forces.

The word "Jehovah" makes the original idea of male-female as the birth originator for the JE is the male emblem and Hovah is Eve. Keep in mind, in Hebrew, the word "Jehovah" is composed of four letters YOD, HE, VAU, and HE, meaning literally Jeve. The YOD (I) or (Y) has, since the most ancient times, been the emblem of the spiritual active or male principle. So it is in the traditions of India, the letters HE in the Kabbalah represents passive and female.

The VAU signifies lying down copulation in the sacred divine tetragrammation. The final repetition of the H represents the product in sum; the YOD symbolizes the spiritual principle, meaning illegible and active. The three letters Eve represent the passive multiple substance-triplicate-whence comes emanation and which must re-enter into the original unity.

The books of Hermes beautifully observe the number (1) one. It is born from the spirit. The phallus one and the yoni zero forms the number (10) ten, which includes all the figures in mathematics. The number 10 is also symbolized in the Roman Numerals by the X (or cross) and the upright with the ovai placed sideways forms the +. This is also the mundane cross of Heaven repeated on earth by plants and dual-man. The physical man supersedes the spiritual at this junction point of which astronomically stands the mythical Libra, Hermes, and Enoch. The faithful man is placed between as the heavenly rescuing shield.

When woman was pulled from the left rib of

Adam, the pure Virgo is separated. It falls into generation (a downward cycle) and becomes an emblem of sin and matter.

Let the student also note that the word "Mater" means *Mother* in almost every language and in like manner we have the terms: Madra, Mat, Mod, Mud, and Matter. The Thyrus, or pinecone, carried in the ancient processions was also emblematical of the male principle. The erect oval window containing the picture of the Virgin (the female principle) of nature becomes the Vesica Pisces and frame for divine things. The Crux Ansata, sign of Venus, testifies the union of the male and female principles in the most obvious manner.

All of our Christian churches contain the symbol of the phallus in their Obelisks or Spires angularly pointing to the Heavens equally as with the Druids in their Ancient circles. David performs his phallic dance before the ark emblem of the female principle. The Hindu Vishnavit bears the same emblem upon his forehead. The spiritual element is marked throughout every religion on earth, and the fleur de lis of France signifies the same.

All architecture is derived from the two mathematical lines the (|) and the (-), which, united and intersecting form the cross. The first is the origin of the upright tower, pyramid, steeple, or male phallic emblem, which aspires against the force of gravity.

The second horizontal mark is the symbol of the tabernacle, chest, ark (or base-line matter). It is the expression of all ancient Egyptian, Grecian, and Jewish Templar Architecture. The union of the two lines give the cross the blending of the two dispensation (law and gospel).

The Argha is ark (or arche) is the Navis Bifrora and has the form of the female crescent which is the woman deity. This is also the Argha of the Hindus and the Arghe was also an oblong vessel used by the high priests as a Sacrificial Chalice in the worship of Isis.

The Ancients placed the Astral soul of man, the psyche, in the pit of the mind. In like manner, the Patera, or cup, was a mystic feminine of Pater, the father. It indicated a lotus-shaped cup, or Matrix. The Patera is a cognate of Pater Patricius, who wore a lunar or crescent-shaped shoe.

The chief of the scared college was called Pater Patratus, which is contracted from Patera. Pater and the spirit are symbolized by the word Patri-Arche, or Patriarch. The word "Peter" in Phoenician and

Chaldaic or P.T.R. literally means the Old Aramaic. In Hebrew, Pater can also be traced to a similar symbolism SS in the noble order of the Garter, which includes the same symbols and the very motto interpreted correctly is "YONI SOIT QUI" and not as erroneously interpreted "HONI."

The origin of the order of the Garter is very different to that which is usually assigned to it; it is an Imperial and feminine order, having its origin in the rose and of a certain and periodical and physiological fact connected with woman's life. The Garters are double red and white; the 26 knights represent the double 13 lunation or the thrice twenty-six mythic dark and light changes in the year.

The round table of King Arthur, the symbolical female discus, in certain mythical aspects is a perfect display of the same subject and King Edward III chose the octave of the purification for the inauguration of his order.

As previously remarked, Mars is the red planet. Purple or red is the ancient mark of initiation, hence the setting aside of this color for the robes of kings and emperors of popes and cardinals or British royalty. This is also true of university degrees from the same dual principle so often referred to originate the white and red roses of English history. White and red banners of the sons of Mars in the Army are also true.

The presiding deity of Ireland is the mystic woman born from the great deep or the fecundity of nature. This is she who is impaled or crucified upon the Tree of Life. The Irish Harp and her hair are entwined into the mystical Seven Strings. We have also the Venus Days, or woman's day/Friday of the seven-fold weekly period and the unlucky marriage day.

The two-table of stone with rounded top placed side by side as a united stone upon the altars of our churches typify the same ideas. They contain the five commandments of the law or man to the right. The pillar of JACHIN and the five of the Gospel to the left woman or the pillar of BOAZ. The right stone is masculine, and the left is feminine.
The Crescent Moon and Star of the Orient has the Star issuing from between the two horns emblem of Ali amongst the Muhammedans is also the symbol of the same ideas in Egypt and Persia, as well as in the House of Plantagent.

We must also strictly keep in mind that there is a higher meaning veiled in those Crescent symbols, for they represent the union of the triad with the unit. The horns of the cow on the head of Isis have precisely the same signification. The Phrygain Cap sanguine in its color with the bonnet rouge, or cap of Liberty, is of precisely a similar origin which has descended to us from the mystic rite of the cirumcisio praeputi.

The Cardinals red hat follows the same idea. It is a Chapeau discus, a mystic feminine rose. We have also the Pall Pallium Pelisse from pellis skin coat, a full reminder of the very remote cover of shame of Adam and Eve and of Noah and Ham. In the Maypole, we again have phallus and yoni with the former wreathed with the seven prismatic colors.

In the same connection, it may be stated that water represents the duality of the Macrocosm and Microcosm, in conjunction with the vivifying spirit and the evolution of the little world from the Universal Cosmos. In Christian Theosophy, it also signifies the mysterious symbol of soul by the interaction of which with the human body man regenerate is born-again to all things pure.

We are all steps in the ladder of progress and we must commence our ascent from the bottom. The spiritual and love nature are the foundation of our existence; for it is so ordered that man's greatest physical happiness, as well as his greatest woes, all spring from this source. If there is something of impurity about it, it is in the mind of him or her who so estimates it.

Of all acts, the spiritual is the most potent as man approaches the very portals of divine creative energy here in the uterus. It is the veiled temple of a woman's body. God baptizes matter with spirit, and behold, it becomes an immortal being. An embryo then has all the powers of the Godhead. God has made nothing of which man may be ashamed for in this soul meets soul, an ecstatic blending of spirit and an ever-watchful deity bending low from on high broods over the Holy of Holies in the temple. The deity also accepts the sacrifice consumed with fires of love.

Entering in is born of woman and the Immaculate Conception is the result of Elevated Souls and a perfect union of such. The resulting child—this truly Love Child—must of necessity be superior to the parents for such is Christ, the Son of the Living God, not of a dead one. Dead gods produce demi-men and women, or devils in human form.

A virgin typifies the purity of soul, and the Holy Ghost is the Holy Spirit. Now the union of such produces the only begotten Son of God, for God cannot be incarnated in impurity and saved as a Progressive Being. The vague legend of the Fall of Man has a sure foundation in truth, for it belongs to every race and every nation. The Fall of Man was the fall of the soul from its perfect (spherical) form to a diffused atomic state.

Man, before he was encased in matter, had no use for limbs but was a pure spiritual entity. As his physical body became heavier, there came the necessity for limbs and such limbs sprouted. The soul, like the perfection of the spiritual sun, was a globe for all organic forms. They are necessarily a complex assemblage of lines and circles, having within his own being all the details in mathematical ratio and the first means of its evolution or the capability of producing and reproducing it.

This earthly state of existence is of necessity, and is just as sacred and paramount a theme as that of the formation of worlds themselves, as the human form of creation is the highest and most wonderful. The mind can then invest deity. The Imitative Law must become the noblest) and most sacred function of God's creatures.

In process of time, the Instinctive Appetites of man's depraved nature stimulated spiritual-worship into excess and thus degraded the noble theme into the grossest licentiousness. Physical generation is the gate by which the soul enters the stupendous pathway of eternal progress. But like all other scared ideas, if abused, the law of such comes to be regarded as mere physical enjoyment and gross sensuality. Hence the necessity which the wise philosophic sages the ancestors perceived of veiling all such teachings on the mysteries in parables and symbolism in our ancient biblical records and other writings.

Childless women were branded with the bitterest reproach Eunuchs and persons afflicted with spiritual blemishes were forbidden to hold sacred offices. This was a law, which descended even to the Roman Catholic popes.

A perfect soul has the emotions perfectly subject to the will, and any part of his system may be affected in any manner desired without provocation of contact with any such objects. However, intercourse prevented her a materialized spirit from returning to her subjective condition. Woman is the offspring of man's own impure fancy; she is created

by an unclean thought. She sprang into existence at
the evil Seventh Hour when the supernatural had
passed away and the natural world began evolving
along the descending Microcosm or the arc of the
great cycle.

Man had unwittingly endowed her with his
own share of spirituality and she became his savior.
When the soul fell to its atomic state, subjective
things became objective and a contact of things
became necessary to produce emotions of pleasure
and pain.

Adam required no contact in spiritual
intercourse to produce ecstasy. Such could be
produced by will with no loss of virility; hence, the
command was that he should not copulate. Disease,
pain, and death itself springs from an abnormal action
of love, for the Fall of Man is a fall of blood. Virility,
for the student, must be turned upward and inward
instead of allowing it to flow outward and downward
in the commission of what St. John terms sin.

Loss of virility is sin and this was the sin,
which lay at the door of Onan (Genesis 38:9). Again,
we find sin lieth as a copulatrix at the door, and is not
only to lie down but also to copulate.

A plant or tree grows up out of the mud, but

a flower and fruit descends. Plants, flowers, fruits, living things, etc., do not ascend out of the ground any more than the sunlight does and we die that others may have being. As the Kabbalists truly say, the lost man (Adam) should have never yielded to the irresistible fascinations of Eve. To the outside world, this is in parables, because it is a part of the secret unwritten Kabbalah, which can be explained only to the Chosen One's man thus evolved out of himself, the woman, as a spiritual entity. He can create no more by his will or spirituality; he can only gain his former condition by a long imprisonment in the bonds of matter.

In the Hebrew text, we have the union of sons of God with daughter of men who were fair viz; one race of purely physical creatures, another purely spiritual for the union of those who produced a third (the Adamtic race), which shared the nature of both its parents.

"I will greatly multiply thy sorrow." Any conception was a spiritual penalty for women because of the fall. Through the virgin soul must come immortality, for salvation is woman's work. As a virgin, neither birth nor conception can take place without first the shedding of blood. This was the fruit

of that forbidden tree, which brought death, as well as life, into the world.

In the future grand cycle under the Prince of the Astral Light, woman will become man's just and lawful equal and intuition will show itself the SUPERIOR of mere intellect. Women truly are a mystery. Jesus, who was never anointed but once then by a woman, of to whom he replied, "She did it for my burial."

It's significant that the races of animated beings turn their eyes downward in spiritual intercourse, but the human family is the exception for man-frail child of matter turns imprisoned himself. The mental state of man looks upwards toward the celestial canopy; for she is saved by child-bearing, for an immortal being is launched upon the infinite Universe of Deity.

The Onanist sees, in his imagination, the object of his lust and thus acting upon his emotions pollutes himself. This wasted virility—though lost to the man, is not lost to nature. It is protoplasm from which springs worms, reptiles, etc. These creatures are a curse to the earth.

Mankind must keep his heart young, tender and full of love for his companion. Think of her as when you wooed and won her, and a passionless man is an infernal monster not only in this but also in all the starry worlds of space. In order to destroy physical or sensual love, think of it in connection with something disgusting and low and it will speedily die. To gaze at a human body, the creature of nine months gestation with repulsive worms crawling in and out of its nine gates.

Chapter 5 | The Cycle Periods of the Great Life-Wave of Material and Spiritual Evolution

As stated before: one Polar Day, which is also the cycle of duration of any life-wave on our planet, is measured by the common years of our earth time— exactly 2,592,000 years. Although the seven planets of our chain vary in the length of their respective life-wave (some a few thousand years more and some a few thousand less), they are on the average all of the same duration.

Hence, the great period of the life-wave traveling once around our centenary chain of worlds is 2,592,000 multiplied by 7 or 18,144,000 years. This is for the complete circuit of seven orbs but the cycle of the life-wave from its leaving the earth to its reappearance is 2,592,000 less than the above. In other words, it is exactly 15,552,000 years.

This period of evolution equals 49 root races of immortal beings, and each race contains its own immortals. This is the period of the life-wave passing seven times around the chain, totaling 127,008,000 years.

For the 50th period, that is the day when those purified souls enter nirvana as a family. This nirvana lasts until the human life-wave has passed around the chain in a passive state and reached the shores of our planet again, or 18,144,000 years.

Each family or new Angelic Planetary state of lately exalted human souls rules the corresponding family upon earth. Thus, the first family, or that which formed the first seven root races after their cycle rules the first seven root races of their new creation and so on with the others.

These new races of human beings evolve and pass through the same harmonious process of evolution from spirit to matter and back to spirit, thus, completing the great cycle of necessity. The planet itself is not recreated after each earthly nirvana (or the peace of God), but re-awakened into activity and life to pass through 127,008,000 years after the period has again expired. This race of guardians also ascend to higher planes and the second planetary family enjoys the peace of God for 18,144,000 years.

THE FIVE GREAT YUGS

(Satya Yug) 1,728,000 years, 4 periods - units = 18 and 9

(Treta Yug) 1,296,000 years, 3 periods - units = 18 and 9

(Dvapara Yug) 864,000 years, 2 periods - units = 18 and 9

(Cali Yug) 432,000 years, 1 period - units = 9

(Muha Yug) 4,320,000 years, 10 periods - units equal = 9

If the student goes over the above numbers, he or she will notice that they are all part of the Divine Age. The Maha Yug is composed of the Cali Yug. For instance: Satya Yug, or four periods, is just four Cali Yugs, and so on. The Cali Yug is the period of the earth's pole passing over 60 degrees of its orbit and thus forming the sex-tile to its own true place.

The Dvapara Yug is the period of the earth's pole forming the trine aspect to its true place and passing over 120 degrees of its orbit. The Treta Yug is the period of the earth's pole passing over 180 degrees of its orbit and forming the opposition to its own place. It is the cycle that rules the day and night, and the evening and the morning of one Polar Day of creation.

Lastly, the Satya Yug is the period of the earth's pole passing over 240 degrees of its orbit. It is the double trine, or double 120 degrees. It is also the cycle that rules the great turning point of the life-wave of the planetary chain. That is when the earth has passed through a Satya Yug, or the culminating point. Life impulse begins to pass to the next planet.

Again, you must observe the regular Harmonious Progression of the terminating units of each Yug 2, 4, 6, 8 and of the periods (Cali Yug) 1, 2, 3, 4. These are the locks, and each one points esoterically to the mysterious hidden number so carefully veiled from the rude gaze of the profane mind.

This sacred guarded number constitutes the Golden Key; it is the Magical 9, and the highest unit. It is a triune, or the highest unit. It is 3x3, which = 9. This is 360 less than 3x9, which = 27 degrees. Its second aspect shows the magical number of Abracadabra (or 666), which is 18, and equals 9.

This sacred number is the perfect symbol of deity. Multiply it as you'd like by any number and it resolves itself into 9. Just as all the different aspects of the eternal and divine essence eventually return into the one primordial source, so does this number no matter to what power it is raised, it's ultimate is 9, hence it is the Divine Figure that can alone unlock the cycles of the Great First Cause.

Keep in mind: the pole passing 60 degrees of its orbit is symbolized by the sun within a six-pointed star. The serpent enfolds a six-pointed star in its coils. The Trine aspect is likewise a Trine, but also as a three-pointed star having three rays. The pole opposition, or passing 180 degrees, is in one of the aspects of the eight-pointed star in which each ray is opposite another. The period of 240 degrees Polar Motion is symbolized by the sun being enclosed in Solomon's Seal. As we know—120 + 120 = 240.

Having explained the preliminary details of the Hindu System, we must now enter upon a more beautiful series of calculations of esoteric cycles and it is necessary in order to comprehend this to reveal the secret period of what the Hindoos termed a Divine Year. This year consists of exactly 360 (9) common years, or the number of degrees in the zodiac. With this year, the ancients used to veil their more treasured cycles.

We will now compare, side-by-side, the five Great Yugs with their esoteric periods when expressed by Divine Years:

(Statya Yug) 1,728,000 = 4 periods / 4,800 divine years

(Treta Yug) 1,296,000 = 3 periods / 3,600 divine years

(Dvapara Yug) 864,000 = 2 / 2,400 divine years

(Cali Yug) 432,000 = 1 period / 1,200 divine years

(Maha Yug) 4,320,000 = 10 periods / 12,000 divine years

First, we see that divine Maha Yug is composed of 12,000 divine years. This constitutes the 10 Great Ages. Secondly, the divine years run 4, 3, 2, 1 and 8, 6, 4, 2 and taken by themselves are:

1,200 or 1 and 2 equal 3; 2,400 or 2 and 4 equal 6; 3,600 or 3 and 6 equal 9; and lastly 4,700 or 4 and 8 equal 12, which are 3, 6, 9, 12.

We explain all these simple matters to show that all the sacred numbers of the Hindoos are one complete and harmonious progression of the nine units.

Please note: the 10 Ages (or Cali Yugs) are also in the East, shown under this symbol of the 10

Avatars.

Chapter 6 | Seven Planetary Governors

In carrying our investigation into the past ages, it will suffice if we begin in the year 1200 B.C. when the Angel of Saturn resumed the government of the world. From the year 1200 B.C. to the year 897 B.C., the earth was under the melancholy influence of the Angel of Saturn. In the very first year of his reign, Troy (the famous Trojan City) was taken and destroyed by the Greeks. Many other events faithfully indicate the nature and power of Saturn's influence.

The Angel of Jupiter became regent of the world and here we note the remarkable difference between the two governors. In the beginning of this angel's reign, Rome, the mistress of the world, was built and the foundation of the mighty empire was substantially laid. All nations began to progress rapidly into a more advanced state of civilization and cultivated the ARTS and SCIENCE.

The Angel of Jupiter was in power from 897 B.C. to the year 588 B.C., and then came the Angel of Mars, who reigned from 588 B.C. to 280 B.C. This period is one of war (Martial Heroes) and brilliant achievements on the field of battle. A glance at the history of Greece and Rome will suffice to show how true this is. After the Angel of Mars came, the Shining Chief of the Seven Intelligences ruled the world from the year 280B.C. to the year 29 A.D.

During this period, most nations attained the climax of power and civilization toward the close of his reign. This bright angel presented the Nations of the West with a teacher who rivaled in moral teachings and excelled in practical benevolence. This teacher was styled by his followers "the Son of God" and was called the Son of God astrologically because he was born into the world during the reign of the Archangel, Micheal.

After Micheal came the Angel of Venus and Love, who ruled from A.D. 29 to A.D. 337. These were the days of religious persecution, and the days of faith and love among the Christians for the doctrine of their noble chief.

Christians loved one another but alas, it was also a time of great licentiousness in Rome when women lusted and participated in debauchery. This period will show the student the two opposite power or forces of Venus's Influence. When exerted for evil, it is all that is obscene and disgusting, but when exerted for good, it evolves that which is noble, elegant and true.

After the Angel of Venus, the Angel of Mercury commenced to rule and was governor, in A.D. 646. At the end of that same year, the Angel of the Moon became the supreme ruler and reigned until A.D. 1263, and made things worse. This included Pagan Darkness and Gross Superstition. The lowest point in the Mental Arc was reached and Western Nations were in the most dence conditions, but a change was at hand. The Angel of Jupiter resumed management of the world and reigned until A.D. 1572.

This period is one of almost uninterrupted intellectual progress during this rule of power. The Despotic Power of Rome received its death-blow; Parliaments were instituted for the people the days of Good Queen Bees came to an end (Protestantism Flourished), and so prepared the way for free thought.

After the Angel of Jupiter, the Angel of Mars came into power and reigned from A.D.1572 to A.D. 1880 until December 21, 1880 when the sun reached the Tropics of Capricorn. Archangel Micheal began to reign on December 23. This rule was the Age of Iron and just as Rome conquered all before her over 2,000 years before and achieved Imperial greatness, so did Great Britain, the second Rome. It was again a period of war, mechanical inventions, and Martial Glory. At times, the whole of Europe was one great battlefield and resounded with the din of arms and all the circumstances of war.

At the end of the year 1880, the great Archangel Micheal comes into power and once more has the government of the world until the year A.D. 2188. This will be a period of Imperial Greatness. Empires will shine full of glory. The Human Intellect will be pronounced. During the reign, the Masculine Element will receive the Solar Influx and obtain its highest development. Intellect and reason will remove most of our social disorders and women receive more attention in worldly affairs but at the same time it is not a feminine period by any means.

Mankind, under this rule, will become physically and intellectually superior to what they are now, by starting discoveries in Chemistry, electricity, and all the physical sciences will be brought to light. Steam will be superseded by compressed air gas electro-magnetism (atomic power) as a motive power. In fact, a new era of progress will dawn upon the world as time and space will be annihilated by new transportation and communication. Last but not least, science and religion will become blended.

The prince of the Astral light will receive the Guardianship of the world and reign from the year A.D. 2188 to the year A.D. 2497.

This the feminine period and woman will, during the Prince of the Astral light's reign, become man's just and lawful equal (socially and politically). Intuition will show itself the superior of mere intellect and the human form physically attaining its greatest degree of perfection. Spiritualism will be taught in our universities.

After the Prince of the Astral Light, this will be the Grand Era of the Mind and the Age of the Genius of Humanity. The culminating point of this cycle is about the year A.D. 2800, or six years before the expiration of the Angel of Mercury's rule in 2806.

The Angel of the Moon, the Seventh Governor, now takes up the reins of power and rules from the year A.D. 2806 to the year A.D. 3114. This rule is again the Stagnation of Mind. Humanity attains the greatest height possible.

Chapter 7 | Naronia

The Naros, or Neros, is the Luni-Solar period in which the moon completes a whole number of lunation in precisely 600 years. The latest example of this, of course, was the revival of true spiritualism in 1880. There is a moment frequently recurring wherein men and women can call down to the celestial-almost great powers from the spaces there being wholly able to reach the souls of others. They can hold them fast in the bonds of a love unknown as yet in this cold land of ours, and to the father that every husband and wife on earth would use it then would this be a far more blessed life to lead.

At birth, a person is endowed with the germs of New Forces, Virtues, Powers, Potencies and Deific Attributes. These are, in some way, renewed annually when the moon, in its monthly course, arrives at a certain unspecified place. It "impregnates" and "vivifies" these germs and enables one to actually acquire the full powers inherent in the the Dream State of Man.

Thank you for reading! Please contact the author, James Ross, for more information and/or for book club inquiries.

www.ingramcontent.com/pod-product-compliance
Lightning Source LLC
Chambersburg PA
CBHW021512210526
45463CB00002B/994